Using Sandvox®

A step-by-step guide to creating your own

website on your Mac

George L. Strout

DEDICATION

To Pat- Thank you for your encouragement and support.

ACKNOWLEDGMENTS

I am very appreciative of all the information and support I have received from Karelia Software and A2 Hosting.

TABLE OF CONTENTS

Introduction

This edition focuses on the latest version of Sandvox as of this writing. Every effort has been made to keep up to date with Karelia's revisions and additions. Verify that you have the current version of the software by visiting the Sandvox website. Karelia tries to stay current with the latest Apple operating system enhancements.

By following the process described in this book, you will create your own website and be ready to publish to the web by the end of Chapter One. Subsequent chapters will lead you through the publishing process and offer suggestions for expanding and customizing your site. You may want to visit the Karelia website for more ideas.

To see a website built following this book, visit http://glstrout.net/ or enter **glstrout.net** into your browser's search window. Explore all the pages on this site for an idea of possibilities for your own site.

Why build a website?

There are as many reasons to build a website as there are people. Businesses want one to create brand recognition and identity and to generate interest and traffic to their service or product. Unfortunately, it can cost thousands of dollars to hire a web designer and pay him or her to be your webmaster and administer your site. For people who operate small independent businesses, that cost can quickly get out of reach. Today, that is no longer a barrier to having a professional presence on the World Wide Web. For less than one dollar a day, you can create and maintain your website and give your enterprise a professional face to the world.

For the individual, there are also many ways to benefit from having a website. If you are self-employed or an independent contractor, having a website can give you a more professional appearance. A nicely designed website can also be a wonderful way to keep in closer contact with people located around the world. Families with friends and offspring in the military or in college can share daily events easily with one another on a dedicated website. Organizations which share common interests with others may enjoy a website devoted to their interest, be it art, photography, writing, fishing, boating, or stamp collecting. Churches and missions share updates with members through websites. Small towns, chambers of commerce, and summer friends at the lake all have the ease of using a website to stay in touch. It's rewarding and easy to do, and Sandvox® makes it easier than ever. Let's get started.

After iWeb®

This is the second book in a series of Web Design books. The first book is a step by step guide to creating your own website using iWeb®, Apple's proprietary program for web design. Currently, the future of that easy to use application is in doubt. A powerful alternative to Apple's program is Karelia

Software's Sandvox®. If you have used iWeb®, Sandvox® will feel comfortable and familiar with a similar user interface and some exciting new features.

Apple has announced that it will shut down MobileMe® in June of 2012 and, as of this writing, it is not clear if they will update or abandon iWeb®. When the latest version of the Mac Operating System, Lion, was released in mid 2011, there was an update of iWeb® released at the same time.

If you are currently using iWeb® on your Mac computer, you can continue to use it for updating your existing website as long as you are hosting it on some other server besides MobileMe®. In any case, by June of 2012, you will have to decide how to proceed with your website. There is a good argument for setting up your site on the new server sooner rather than later and posting a message to redirect people to your new website on the existing MobileMe® address so people can find your new location.

Built into iWeb® is the choice of publishing your site to a local folder, MobileMe® or to an outside site by using FTP (File Transfer Protocol). The FTP option allows you to continue to use the iWeb® program to update and maintain your site. See the list of hosting services for more choices. Most of the hosts listed will guide you through the process of moving your site to their server using iWeb®.

There is a publishing alternative using the local folder setting and the Drop Box on your computer but I recommend you avoid that because it requires you to leave your computer on and accessible at all times. The Internet Service Provider is better able to do this for you and the cost is very reasonable and competitive on most servers.

The purpose of this book is to offer an alternative to iWeb® and to provide a quick, easy guide to creating or moving your website. We will explore the options and build a website using Sandvox®. The photos and descriptions in this book are from the actual process I followed. If you follow these steps, you will have an operating website at the end of Chapter One. It will guide you through the design and development of a website. Chapter Two will show you how to publish your site. Chapter Three will deal with finding and signing up for a web hosting service and registering your own domain name (yourname.com). The subsequent chapters will explore and explain all the features of Sandvox®.

Using this book

As we work though this book, the tabs or commands you will need to find and interact with are in **bold**. Whenever you see a **bold** item, you should find the same word in the Sandvox® App. This will be the command you will use in that step.

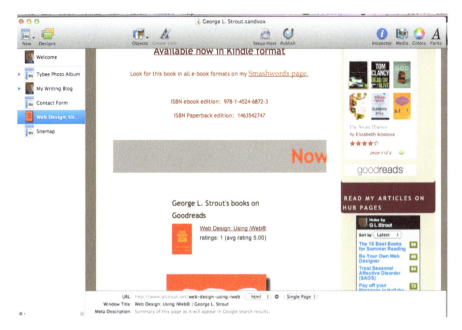

Throughtout the book you will find screenshots of the project we are working on at that point. By matching your developing web site to the photo, you can be sure your project is on track.

A word about Copyright

Remember, when you post your website on the Internet, you are publishing. You are subject to all the same rules and restrictions any professional newspaper or magazine publisher would have to follow. Be sure you own the rights to whatever you include in your website or that you have permission to post the item. Also be sure to give credit for those items which are not yours just as you would want credit for your work on someone else's website.

1 Creating your website

By the end of this chapter, you will have an operating website that you have designed. Subsequent chapters will give you enhancements and alternatives to expand and maintain your site.

We will use a program called Sandvox® Website Creator by Karelia Software. The reasons for using Sandvox® are:

• Sophisticated and familiar layout very much like iWeb®
• Large selection of themes and tools
• Easy publishing options
• Extensive help and user support
• A large selection of third party enhancements
• Intuitive user interface

Getting Started with Sandvox®

If you have used iWeb®, the transition will be nearly seamless and if you have never designed a website, the program is very intuitive. As of this writing, you can download a free trial copy of Sandvox®. This will allow you to try out the program and create pages for your website before you decide to buy the program. You will be able to publish up to five pages of your website before you buy the program.

If you want to try the free trial, go to: http://www.karelia.com/Sandvox/ and download it from there. Follow the simple installation process and you are ready to go. You can also download the software from the Mac App Store but you will not get the free trial.

Step by Step

Now we will begin to create your web site. Follow the process described below.

Once you have installed the program, launch it and you will be greeted by the Welcome screen. Click on the play button and watch the screencast to get a basic introductory orientation to the program. You will be introduced to the toolbar, site content menu and shown how to add and edit a page. After watching the video, we will go a bit slower and work with each section to understand all the features.

Sandvox® Welcome Screen

Go to the Sandvox® menu across the top of your screen, and choose **File>New Site**. You will be presented with the

Design Menu that contains over 50 predesigned themes. Take a moment to browse through the variety and choose one that reflects your personality and the mood you want to convey on your new website. For this tutorial, I am choosing "Expansion." The new page will automatically fill in some information when it creates the first web page. You will be able to edit these elements as needed. While the App will automatically save a backup, remember to save your changes you want to keep periodically.

Here is the page as it appears on my computer with my name pre-populated along with other Sandvox® information. We can change all of that at any time.

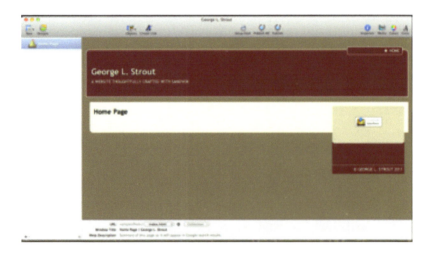

New design page

The column to the left is the Site Outline or content list which will list each page as we add them. For now, change the phrase under the name from "A WEBSITE THOUGHTFULLY CRAFTED WITH SANDVOX" to "HAVING FUN BUILDING A WEBSITE". Highlight it with your cursor and type the new phrase. Notice that, as your cursor passes over the page, boxes appear. These are Text Boxes.

Next, highlight the word "PAGE" in the phrase "HOME PAGE". Delete the word "page" and notice that the title in the left side Site Outline also changes to "Home." This is your page title and the left side menu (site outline) will show whatever you name the page here.

As you move your cursor over the page, the various text boxes will appear as an outline. Place you cursor just below the box that surrounds the word Home and you can start adding your own text to the page. Write a brief introductory paragraph welcoming people to your site. While we are doing this, let us change the word "Home" to "Welcome."

Now, our page should look something like this:

Our new Welcome Page

The little graphic symbols will be explained later. For now, look at the text box to the right of the page where the Sandvox® logo is. Go to the top menu bar to **Insert** and scroll down and click on **Text Box**. A large untitled box will appear just above the logo. It contains gibberish to hold a place for your text. Highlight the header (UNTITLED TEXT) and type in "My Favorite Quote." Next, highlight the nonsense text below that and type in a quote you like.

Changing Fonts

Now is a good time to improve the look of your page by choosing a font and style of type you like. Every theme is set with a default font. You can change the font in any text box by selecting that box, choosing "select all" under the edit menu and then choosing

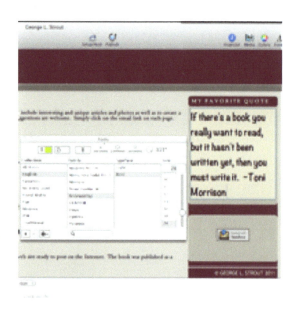

the font you want. In the Sandvox® menu bar just above the page, is a large letter *A* with the word "**Fonts**" below it. Click on this and the font menu will open. For now, scroll down the center menu under "Family" and choose a font you like. If you left the text highlighted it will show you what the new font will look like on the page. Experiment with style and size also, until you find what you like. You can always come back and change it later. For this tutorial, I chose "Noteworthy, bold, 24."

All text and fonts appear on your website in a text box. Later, we will learn how to add and edit them.

Changing Themes

Now is a good time to try different themes. On the menu just above your new web page, is an icon labeled "**Designs**". By opening the design menu, you can choose any of the available designs and it will show you how this page will look in the new theme. Take a few minutes to try some that interest you and choose the one you like. In most cases, whatever changes we make will apply to any of the designs. Alternatively, you can follow the steps in this book through to the end of Chapter One using the "Expansion" theme and then change to whatever theme you like at the end of Chapter One. This will allow you to match the illustrations in this book.

Adding a Banner

Banners are a special element. Not all themes have banners. In the Sandvox® Designs menu, the banners will normally appear as a placeholder photo behind the website title. Those that contain banners will allow you to change the photo or background to personalize the site. This change will affect every page on your site. Go to the **inspector tool, i,** under Document and click on **Appearance**; if a banner is possible on the theme you chose, the drop down menu under Banner will be available. If it is not available, your design does not use a banner and you can skip to the section on adding a new page or try a different design.

Changing the Banner

At the top of the page, the name of the website appears in a solid color background. This is a banner that extends across the page and can be changed.

> **User Tip:** For now, choose a photo from your iPhoto library to use as a banner. For future convenience, create a new album in iPhoto and file all the images you use in your website in one place. This will allow you to come back later and edit or change them.

In your photo program choose a photo and save it to the desktop where you can easily find it. For a banner, you may want to use a photo of clouds or water or some subject that presents a good background. The banner will tend to default to the top third of the photo. You may want to edit the photo to fit the space or give a more attractive appearance. Your photo program, such as iPhoto®, will provide cropping and centering tools. See your photo application for instructions on editing.

- Once you have the image you like, open the inspector menu (the blue "*i*" in the menu bar) and choose the first icon. It will be titled **"Document"** at the top of the inspector.
- Now choose "**Appearance**" from the button just below the top. You will now see a drop down menu that gives you a choice of "design-supplied" or "image fill."
- Choose **image fill** from the drop down menu; then choose the photo on your desktop and it will appear on your web page.
- Once you have done this, you can change the image by repeating the step above.
- Drag your edited image to your new "Website Photos" file or iPhoto® album.

Personalizing

Now, you can add some personal information to your website. We will use the sidebar and the text box functions. Go to the **Objects** icon in the menu bar and choose **Text Box**. A new Untitled Text box will appear at the top of the sidebar. You can change the title to "About" by highlighting "untitled text" and typing in the new title.

If you would like to put a photo in the About box, open the **Media** tool and drag the photo you want to the area where you want it.

> **User Tip**: If you resize a photo in iPhoto® a photo of about 75 pixels by 98 pixels will fit nicely in the sidebar. Alternatively, using the little boxes on the edges of the photo, you can size it to fit.

Arrange your text the way you like. You will notice that the text box automatically sizes to fit the content.

Adding a New Page

Adding a new page to your site is easy and fun. First, we will add a photo album page, then a blog page. Both of these types of pages are called "Collection" pages by Sandvox®. They will appear to have other pages under them in the Site Outline on the left of the Sandvox® window. The first page that appears in each collection in Site Outline is referred to as the "parent" page of that collection. The pages that appear below that, indented on the Site Outline, are the "child" pages. Again, Sandvox® makes it easy and intuitive to create your photo album.

Go to **New** and scroll down to **Photo Album.** When you click on this icon, it will add a new page to the site outline called Photo Album. Beside the new page is a small triangle indicating items contained in this page, but at the moment, no items are shown.

The new page shown in the page view window, contains the same header as your Welcome or Home page, and matches the theme and banner. Any sidebar changes you have made also appear on this page. In the body of the page, is the phrase "Photo Album" and a strange, placeholder photo. To the right of the photo is a gray box with a dashed line around it and the instruction: "Drag images here." Now for some magic: click on the **Media** button at the top right of your screen and open your **Images** library. Scroll through your photos and choose one you would like to represent your new photo album. Drag that image to the gray area on the web page. As soon as you do that, the placeholder photo is replaced by your own photo. Now drag any other photos you want to the area just to the right of the first photo and they will space themselves automatically on the page and the page will grow to fit your album. If you decide you want to remove a photo from the album, highlight it in the **Site Outline** on the left and choose **delete** under the **edit** menu.

To add a title to your photo you can click on the **photo** to see the enlarged version. The name will appear above the larger image; highlight the default text over the photo and type in your new text. It will also appear in the Site Outline beside the small image of the photo.

You will want to give your new album a name that describes the subject. Highlight the words **Photo Album** in the **Site Outline** and type in the new name; hit **enter**. When you do, it will appear in the Site Outline at the left as well as on the top of the main photo album page and in the menu bar for your website. You will not want the same title on each album; it is easy to change this to make each album unique Repeat these steps to create as many collections, or albums as you like. In the following image you will see the Site Outline on the left showing the Welcome page and the new Photo Album page with all the photos I have added below it. To the right is the inspector tool showing the layout options. Your page should look similar to this.

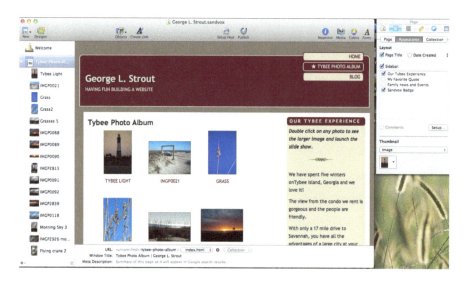

Layout options on a Photo Album page

Changing Text Box Content

Open the inspector menu by clicking on the blue *i*. Be sure you are on the page where you want to change the text box. In the inspector menu, click the second icon at the top, which is the **page** layout. For now, we will deal only with "**Appearance**" so click on the **appearance** button, the second one in the next row of buttons.

Now you are presented with a series of check boxes under the heading "Layout." Take a moment to check and uncheck these boxes to see how they affect your page.

On the welcome page, you created a text box labeled "My Favorite Quote." While you are on the Photo Album page, go to the layout tool; find that label and uncheck it. Then go to **Objects** in the menu bar and click on **Text Box**. A new text box appears on your page ready for you to enter a new message. Give this box a header, which will be the title that shows on the layout inspector tool, and enter your message. At this point, your web page should look similar to the photo on the previous page. By checking and unchecking the item in the list under **Sidebar**, you can choose which items appear in the sidebar on each page. By unchecking the Sidebar title, the entire sidebar will disappear from the page.

Creating a Blog

A blog can be a great way to keep the public interested in your products and projects. On a family website, it is a wonderful way to stay up to date on family news and events. It is also a good outlet for your creativity. In Sandvox®, creating a blog is easy to do.

The blog page is a "Collection" page just like the Photo Album page. To create your blog page, go to **New** and scroll down to **Blog**. As soon as you click on the blog icon, your new page appears in the Site Outline along with the first blog entry page. By default, Sandvox® will open on the first blog entry page, the first "child" page, and not on the blog home (parent) page. In the Site Outline, the blog home page appears as the "parent" page for your blog. There is placeholder text on these pages that you can replace to create your introduction and your first blog entry.

- You can highlight the words "**First Post**" and give it a new title. This will be the first entry in your new blog and *not* your introductory or index page for your blog.
- Move your cursor to the text below the small word "blog", highlight and delete the placeholder text and type in your first

blog entry. The small word "blog" in the middle of the page represents an index that will grow as you make entries.

- Go to the **Site Outline** and choose the "parent" blog page and highlight the title and replace it with your blog name. You might call it "Pearls of Wisdom."

- Place your cursor in the main body of the blog home page (it will appear below your first blog entry) and type your introduction to your blog.

- Now, the first blog entry and the box it is in will be displayed. Drag it below the introduction. Your introduction is now in place and summaries of all entries will appear below it on the home page of your blog.

- For each new blog entry, highlight the blog parent page and select **New>Empty** from the menu and a new child page will appear in your Site Outline.

Blog Page

Now, let us add a contact form so your reader can easily communicate with you. Be sure you have highlighted the Home, or Welcome page of your website. Go to **New>Contact Form** and it will appear below your blog page in the Site Outline. When you look at the page in the preview window, you will see a long gray box with a message telling you to enter your email address in the inspector. Click once on the gray box to highlight it. Open the **inspector tool** and go to the last icon on the right along the top of the inspector window. This is the **Object** inspector. Below the top row is another row of buttons that give you a choice of message and fields. Choose **message** and enter your email address in the space provided in the inspector. For now, leave the fields alone and you can explore that option later.

An alternative way for people to contact you is to put your email address on each page. One way to do this is to create a sidebar link. Use these steps to create a link you can use on any page:

- Under **Objects** select **Text Box.** It will appear at the top of the sidebar. You can drag it anywhere in the sidebar that pleases you.
- In the heading for the text box type in "Contact Me" or whatever you choose.
- In the body of the text box, highlight all the text and type in "Send me an email:". Keep this text highlighted. Open the **inspector** by clicking on the blue *i*. Choose the **link** inspector, the blue curved arrow in the inspector menu. Under the "**Link to:**" drop down menu, choose **email** and it will automatically fill in the email address in your account or

you can type in a different one. Check the "**Make all links active**" box to activate the email link or hold down the shift key while the cursor is on the link to test it.

• Now that you have created this text box, you can add it to any of your pages. Go to the **inspector** and click on the **page inspector**, the second icon at the top, and choose "**Appearance**" from the next menu down in the inspector window. In the list of text boxes under **Sidebar**, choose the boxes you wish to appear on each page.

Now is the time to finalize your site by going back to the **Design menu**. Try different themes on your site. Choose the one you like and arrange the items on your site to give the look you want. Edit and verify the information you have included and add whatever you like. We will add more features and refinements later after the site is published. Once you make your choices, you may want to **save** the changes you have made so that you have a basic website to build on later. Your site is now ready to publish. You will be able to easily make changes and additions to it at any time. As you work in Sandvox, you are actually working on the copy of your site on your computer. The changes will not show on the Web until you re-publish your site. The next chapter will lead you through signing up with a web hosting service and publishing your site.

Notes

2 Publishing your new site

Review your site and check the arrangement and spelling on each page.   Go to **Edit>Spelling & Grammar** for the tools you need. You now have created a basic, unique website. Later, we will expand and enhance it with many options available in Sandvox® but, for now, let us go through the process of publishing it. It is not difficult or expensive.

First you must find a hosting service. Again, Sandvox® makes this easy with a step by step process.

For simplicity, we will follow the lead of Sandvox® and choose to host on a remote location using the A2 Hosting as recommended by Sandvox®. If you already have a hosting service set up, you can still follow these steps. If you have not yet set up a hosting service, go to Chapter 9 for more detailed information on how to sign up for the service and obtain your Domain Name.

For purposes of this tutorial, go to **Setup Host**, and click on the "**Edit**" button. The next page will give you choices for publishing locations. Choose "**On a remote Host.**" We will use A2 because MobileMe is shutting down in June of 2012. Note that there is also an offer for a discount on A2 services. Click on the blue link to A2 Hosting and sign up for the service; then return to this page. A2 will walk you through the process.

Remember to claim your discount and be sure to read all the information they give you.

Now click **continue** back on the Sandvox® page. This page asks for the internet information you will need to upload your website. Your hosting service will provide this for you. A2 will email this information to you.

Enter the URL where your site will reside. For example, http://www.yourname.com

- Enter the host name which the hosting service will give you. It will be similar to wwwxx.a2hosting.com "XX" will be a number that A2 will assign you.

Your upload method should be SFTP if possible because it is more secure. Talk to your hosting service about this if you have a problem.

Host Setup Window in Sandvox®

- User Name is the name you used as your identifier with your hosting provider.
- Enter the password you used at your hosting service.
- The document root will also be provided by the host service. It will look something like /home/yourname/public_html
- You will probably not have a subfolder.

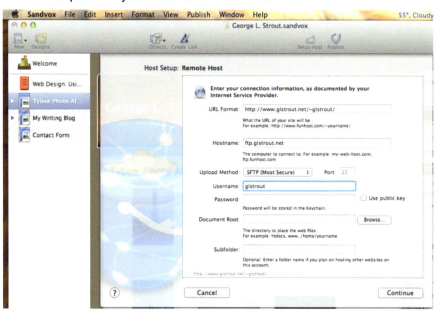

Completed publishing setup page

Now click "**continue**," and Sandvox® will test your setting and confirm your connection to the server.   Once all the settings are correct, your site will be uploaded to the web. If you have any problems with this process, contact the hosting service for help. They can provide the specific information for your site.

Congratulations on publishing your new site. Now send notices to all your contacts so they can admire your work.

Notes

3 Exploring Sandvox®: The Menu Bar

Now that you have a working website, you will want to make it more personalized and exciting. We will explore each of the commands and options available on the Sandvox® screen.

Across the top of the main Sandvox® window is a Mac style menu bar. You are already familiar with the **New** icon in the bar. When you hold down your mouse on the **New** icon, a drop down menu appears that lists all of the blank pages available in the theme you are working in at the moment. You can choose from a long list of page styles and layouts to fit your needs.

One thing to note is the choice of adding a new page with or without a sidebar. Remember that the inspector also allows you to add or remove the sidebar on any page as well as choose which modules you include in each individual page's sidebar. There is more on that under the inspector discussion.

There are two unique options that need special explanation. Look at the **External Link** option near the bottom of the list. This powerful tool will allow you to connect your website to another site. If your browser is on the site you are linking to, and you have checked **Read URLs from web browser** the link will appear automatically. You can do this manually by simply adding the URL to this page after you choose it. Again the inspector offers more options for configuring your link. You can choose to have the link open in a new window, have it show in the menu bar, add it to your site map, and make a few other changes. Experiment with your choices but consider whether you want to encourage your visitors to leave your site for another. Perhaps it would be better to simply list the link on your site as a favorite.

The bottom option is the **Choose...** option and it will be discussed later in the chapter on Adding Bells and Whistles. It gives you a powerful tool for adding a file to your site.

The next option across the menu bar is the **Design** icon. You will have had some experience with that by now. This is a good time to take a few minutes to try on different designs with your new website, if you have not already. We are now working on the copy of your site that is saved on your computer. It is like a clone of your site. Remember, you can try different themes and always return to the original design; you are only experimenting on your copy on your computer until you publish. If you want to work on a new version of your site, save it under a new name until you are ready to publish it. Also, in the page inspector, under Publishing, is a check box that allows you to work on a page and not publish until it is ready. Use the **Draft** checkbox to keep your work-in-progress unpublished until you are ready to release it. Now that you have several pages in your website, you can begin to see just how each design looks with your content.

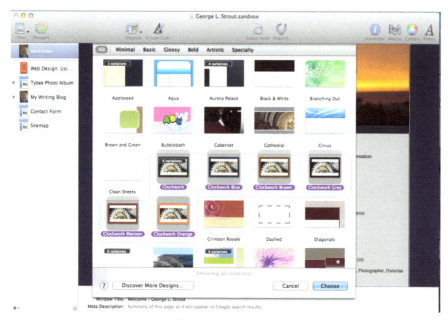

Designs menu

With over 60 built-in designs, and more available from other sources, the possibilities are practically endless. You may want to consider developing your own design using CSS programming. For now, choose a design you like and we will continue the tour of the menu bar.

The Objects menu

The Objects menu contains a number of very powerful and fun options for your site. Some of these items you have already used to build your page.

> **User Tip:** If you have "sidebar" checked and active on your page, the object will usually appear at the top of the sidebar. If you are not using the sidebar feature, the object will appear at the top of the text on your page. You can then drag and drop the object where you want it on the page.

Plan your visitor's experience to achieve the goal you want. If you are selling or promoting something, you may want to try to hold their interest and keep them on your site.

Here is a review of the objects available.

Text Box is an interesting tool. It will work in two different ways. If you have selected a sidebar for your page (see the section on the inspector), when you select "text box" it will appear at the top of your sidebar. You can then move it anywhere you want in the sidebar by dragging it.

If you have not selected a sidebar for your page, the text box will appear on the <u>opposite side of where the sidebar would be.</u> If the sidebar normally appears on the left side of the page, the text box will appear on the right. You can then drag the text box vertically, but not horizontally, to place it where you want on the page. This appears to be true with all designs. If you add a text box then choose the sidebar from the inspector, it is possible to have a text box on one side and a full sidebar on the other side. This leaves you a wide column down the middle for your main text. Again, you can experiment to get the look you like.

Block Quote is a quick, easy way to highlight a key text entry that you might use to promote your product or quote a customer review. It gives you a professional look and drives the viewer's eye to the key point you want to emphasize.

Media Placeholder will give you a spot to drag and drop a movie clip or music snippet to add those features to your site. Put the placeholder where you want it on your page; then drag and drop the movie or music object to it. It will replace the placeholder and automatically be ready to play.

Caution: Be sure you have the right to publish or use the item you place on your website. Most youTube videos and many other sites allow and even encourage you to embed their promotional videos on your site.

Here is an example. Go to http://vimeo.com/ 27312877 . Here you will find a video featuring the Tesla Electric vehicles. One of the options is "embed" which allows you to add this video to your site. Here is how to do that:

• In this case, since they will supply the HTML code to you, go to **Insert>Raw HTML** and drag the HTML placeholder where you want the video to appear.

• If it is not already open, choose **Edit>Raw HTML** and copy the embed code from the video site to the edit window in Sandvox.

• Click on **Update Preview** in the edit window and the video will appear on your page.

With a little experimentation you will discover many ways to use this feature. Also, if you just drag a video or sound item from the media browser to the place where you want it on your webpage, it will load and play.

Indexes can give your site a polished, professional look and aid your visitor in navigating around your site. They are especially useful on pages that are collections such as photo albums and blogs. There are several different versions of indexing objects.

Collection Archive gives you a blog-like index of recent entries and changes to your webpage. If you are writing a blog, it will automatically connect to that collection and you can choose which pages display the object using the sidebar inspector check box.

Photo Grid is another powerful index. If you have already created several pages on your website, selecting this object will automatically create a photo index on your web page. This is very similar to the index that is created when creating a photo album. It can make a nice graphical index on your home page.

Site Map and **Titles & Summaries** are both indexing options that have useful functions but you may find the site map page under the New menu more to your liking. They are handy options to have since you can insert them where you want them. As an aid in getting your site discovered by the search engines, a site map is indispensable. I recommend you include one on your website.

Raw HTML is extremely versatile and you will no doubt use it often when you get comfortable with it. It allows you to insert HTML code where you wish in your web page. It allows you to build connections to other sites and to add features that would otherwise require you to know HTML programming. An example of this function is shown on the next page.

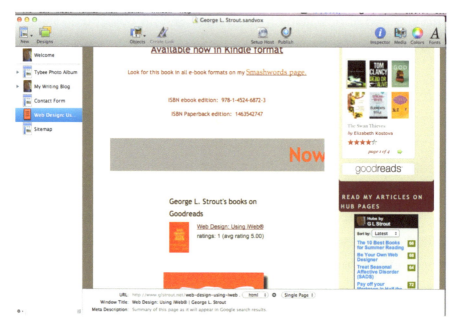

HTML Objects

There are four HTML objects on this page, the scrolling banner, the two Goodreads links and the HubPages box are all HTML inserts that have been copied and pasted from the website they link to. As you can see, this is a convenient way to make your site more interesting and promote links to your products or interests. To learn more about HTML, read the section in Chapter 6 on HTML Snippets.

Amazon List is useful if you have something for sale on Amazon. If you have a book, for example, you can use this object to create a promotional link to your product. If you are an Amazon Associate, you can also get a link from Amazon that will allow you to receive credit for all sales originating from your website. You could also use this object to share some item you are especially enthusiastic about with your family and friends.

Some of the other more significant objects are:

IM Status Inserting this object on your pages will let people know when you are online and available to contact live.

Map will display your location on a Google Map and automatically uses the location you have entered in your personal information. To change the location, go to the **inspector menu** and edit the location information in the **object inspector**. The **inspector** also offers several other options to customize the Google Map the way you want it to appear.

YouTube will link to a YouTube video. Be sure you give credit where credit is due and that you can legally link to the site. In most cases, it will not be a problem if you are sharing a video that you like on YouTube.

Set up Host

If you followed the steps in Chapter 2, you have set up hosting for your site. This section will give you more detailed options for hosting.

Sandvox® makes it easy and fast to manage publishing and updating your website. When you click on the "set up Host" button in the top menu bar of the window, a window will appear telling you "This website is not set up to be published on this computer or on another host." If you are not experienced at setting up a site, you may want to take their advice and read the help screen on this page; click on the question mark in the lower left corner. The information is clear and easy to follow; be sure to read the Sandvox guidelines on hosting. In most cases, you will need to publish to a remote location and, as of June, 2012, MobileMe will not be an option.

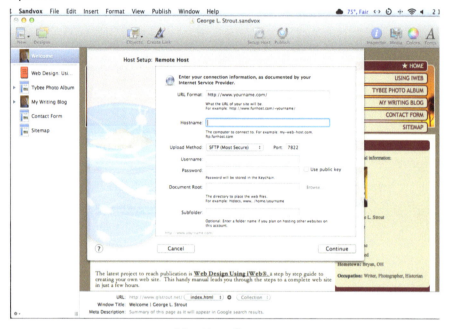

Hosting Setup

Once you have established an account with a hosting service, follow their steps for setting up a host site. There are many hosting services available. A sampling of them are listed elsewhere in Chapter 9. Shop several of them and choose the one you like. In most cases, once the site is up and running, you will probably have little contact with them. Most of your activity will be updating your site as you add new information and update your blogs. Most reputable hosts are quite reliable and easy to deal with. You can find reviews on the web for various hosts.

Domain Name

Before you set up your hosting, consider what you want to do about your domain name. This is your opportunity to have a personalized domain such as www.johndoe.com or www.johndoe.net . If you check with most hosting places they will give you the opportunity to verify that the name you want is available or suggest alternatives to your first choice. In most cases, it will cost little or nothing to get your domain name if you sign up with that service. It should never cost more than $15.00. Another aspect of having a dedicated domain name is the new email address you can have, for example, john@johndoe.com.

Take a few minutes to consider what you want for a domain name and how you expect to use it. Don't make the domain name too long. Once again, you want it to be a memorable name.

- Try to choose a name that is easy to remember and associated with your product in some way.
- Use a name that is easy to spell.
- Consider purchasing multiple forms of your name such as .com, .net, etc., so that others cannot use them.
- Avoid hyphens; users often forget to add them when typing in your address.
- Remember to renew your domain registration when it is due.
- Consider doing a Trademark Search on Google to verify that no one has that name already.

Follow the steps outlined by Sandvox® and click publish when you are ready to go "live" with your new site.

Updating Your Site

Updating your site is easy. Once the initial publishing is done, click the publish button each time you make an alteration to your site in the Sandvox® program. Be sure to save your changes each time.

Notes

4 The inspector tool

This is where you will do most of your editing and manipulation of the web elements. The range and power of this menu is the most important element is Sandvox®. If you have used practically any program on a Mac, you will have some familiarity with inspector menus. One of the advantages to Sandvox® is its affinity with Apple interface elements. Start by clicking on the blue "*i*" on the menu bar. The inspector will open, probably where you do not want it to be. Hold your cursor down on the top of the window and drag the inspector to a place you want.

Site

• By default, Document inspector opens on the "**Site**" tab. In this window, you can enter information such as author name, language and date format. Unless you have a specific reason, do not change the character encoding. The important item here is the **Google Tools** option. This helps the search engines find the content on your website and helps generate traffic. Click on this button. It will open a window with the heading, "Verification" and give you instructions as well as a link to "**Google Webmaster Tools**."

• Click on this link and follow the instructions at Google as well as on this screen. Once you have embedded the verification link, published your site again and successfully confirmed that it worked at Google, follow the instructions for submitting the sitemap.

Google Tools Screen

- Click on the "**Google Analytics**" tab in the Google window on their website.
- Click on the link to Google Analytic and follow the instructions for entering a new website profile. This will generate a code for you to copy and paste into the space provided in Sandvox®.
- Publish your site again and confirm that it is working as it should.
- When you finish, click **Done** and you will have your site registered with Google which will help direct traffic to your website.

Appearance

Under the **Layout** heading, you can check and uncheck the boxes to see how it affects your web page. If you wish to add a logo, check the logo box and a placeholder will appear on your web page. Choose the image you want to use as a logo and drag and drop it on the placeholder.

A *Favicon* is an image associated with a website such as the image that appears in front of the website's URL in the address bar of your browser. You can choose a photo or logo or use the default Sandvox® image. Often, no image will be displayed in the browser but it will show in your Site Outline to the left of the web page window in Sandvox®.

Graphical Title will have different effects depending on which design you are using. In many cases, it will not have any effect and in others, it will allow you to change the appearance of your site's title. Again, remember that any change you make here will apply to your entire site.

The images settings for Sharpness and Quality should be as high as you can set them unless it creates a problem on your browser when loading your pages. Usually this is not a problem.

Page Inspector

The second icon at the top of the inspector bar is the Page inspector. It includes Page, Appearance and Collection tabs. Under the Page tab, you will see a selection of check boxes. The draft check box allows you to work on a new page without publishing it until you are ready. You can continue to keep your blog up to date for example while you work on a new photo album for your site. You do not have to publish the album until you are ready; just keep the draft box checked for the album.

Under the **Navigation** settings, you can choose to open this page in a new window if you want. Most people find this somewhat irritating since it can create multiple layers in the browser.

Include Page In: You can choose to include the page you are working on in the site indexes, menu, and site map by checking and unchecking the related boxes. In most cases you will want to include all three so that the search engines and visitors can easily find the page. If you want to keep a page private, you may want to uncheck these boxes for that page. You will have to send the URL to those people you want to see the page however, because they will not find it on your site otherwise. While the page seems to be "invisible," remember it is still out there in cyberspace so do not include any sensitive or financial information. Someone could still stumble upon it.

The **Link to previous/next** option is only available when working with collections, such as blogs and photo albums. You can choose a graphical or text menu to page through your collections or none at all if you wish.

Meta Tags

Probably the most important item on this inspector page is the Meta Tag box. This is where you enter the terms and words that will help search engines find you and tell them what the contents of your pages are. Consider what you have included on each page and enter the words that best describe

your site. As you enter blog entries and add new pages, be sure to update the meta tags for that page. When you enter the words here, Sandvox® automatically enters the terms into the header for that page so that it is picked up by the search engines. Be accurate so that people find what they expect on your page. By the same token, you want to include all the possible legitimate links to your page. You can read more about Meta Tags on the Sandvox® website under the help menu.
http://www.karelia.com/Sandvox®/help/z/Tags.html

Appearance

The Appearance tab under the Page inspector will probably be the most used tab as you build your site. Each page will become an individual feature of your site through this tool.

Appearance Inspector

You can choose to have a title or date on your page or leave them off. Notice the Sidebar check box. You can choose the sidebar for each page or you can choose to leave it out on an individual page. Try checking and unchecking the sidebar box and see how it affects the appearance of your page. Now, look in the list of sidebar items in the box below the sidebar checkbox. You will see every sidebar item you ever created. If you created an "About Me" text box on your welcome page and it was located in the sidebar, you will be able to choose to use that same text box on any other page in the sidebar simply by checking it. If you prefer, you can only use it on the Welcome page and leave it unchecked on all other pages. You can move the individual text boxes around within the sidebar by grabbing them and dragging them up or down the sidebar on the actual page you are modifying.

To create a new sidebar text box, go to the menu under **Objects** and choose **Text Box**. The new box will appear at the top of the sidebar.

- Highlight the title and type in your title.
- Highlight the nonsense text in the box and enter your message.
- You can also add a photo or Raw HTML Snippet in the text box.
- To enter HTML, place your cursor anywhere in the Sidebar and choose **Raw HTML** from the **Objects** menu. A new Sidebar item will appear at the top of the Sidebar with a title and placeholder for the HTML object.
- Select the box that contains "[[RAW HTML]]" and Choose **Edit>Raw HTML**. Enter the new code snippet. For more

detail, see the section on Bells and Whistles. If you want to learn more about HTML and CSS, go to

http://www.w3.org/

Setting up comments

If you wish to allow people to comment on your website or blog, you will need to set up a comment service to allow control over the process. Again, Sandvox® makes this easy. Click on the button marked "**setup**" and a window will appear. You will be presented with four choices: either none or one of three prepopulated comment services. You will also find a link to the various services to sign up and open an account to moderate your comment feature. If you choose to use Facebook, you will have to verify your account by adding your mobile phone or credit card

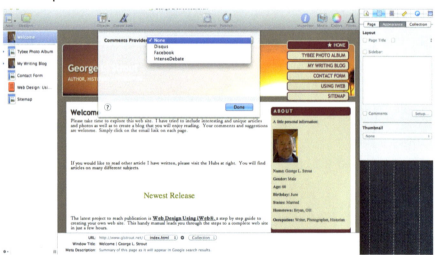

Comments Setup Screen

The other two services will give you a "shortname" to enter in Sandvox® and the rest of the setup is very simple.

To use the comment feature on one of your web pages, check the comments box in the inspector and publish your site. The comment feature will appear at the bottom of your page. You can add this to any page you wish and disable it at any time. By opting to act as moderator, you will need to approve each comment before it appears on your website.

The last item on this inspector tool is **Thumbnail**, which allows you to choose an image that will appear beside the page in the site outline on the left of your screen. This is basically for your benefit to quickly spot the page you wish to edit. Remember, it is the Favicon that appears in the URL line of your visitor's browser.

The next tab under the **Page** inspector is the **Collection** inspector. If you click on this and you are not on a collection page such as a blog or photo album, you will see just one option: **Convert to Collection**. If you are on a collection page, you will be presented with more options. You can set the sorting parameters, the type of RSS feed that fits your collection and choose to publish an archive of your blog or collection which will insert a special text box in the sidebar and automatically update when you make changes. If you have not chosen a sidebar for your collection, it will automatically insert the sidebar if you choose "Publish Archive."

Automatic Sorting

When you highlight the Home or Welcome page in the sight outline to the left of the Sandvox® window, then click on the **Collection** tab under the **Page inspector,** the first option will be the **Automatic Sorting** setting. In the drop down menu, you can choose from four options. This will determine the order in which your pages will appear in the site index. If you choose to set the option "**None**," you will be able to drag and drop the pages in the Site Outline to arrange them in any order you wish.

The **RSS Feed** gives you three options. Normally, the Standard feed will be the best choice. In more advanced situations, the photocast or podcast settings may be useful. In most cases you should not change the filename and you can choose to list an archive; however usually it will be more distracting than helpful.

The **Wrap inspector** is the next tab across the top. This tool works with objects that you can insert into your web page such as a photo. When you click on the object, you will see options for the placement of images and objects in relation to the text on your page. Highlight a photo image on your page or any object such as the YouTube object that will appear in the body of your web page. Now check and uncheck the **Object Placement** buttons to see how it affects your page. You can go under the **Edit** menu and click on **undo** repeatedly to return to your original position or close without saving and reopen the

page to restore it to your last saved page. Once you are comfortable with the behavior of the Object Placement option, arrange your objects the way you like them.

If you choose to have your object "Inline", you will be able to choose how it behaves with your text by clicking on the images in the middle of the inspector window. Again, try the various options and decide what looks best for your site. If you choose "Callout," the image will appear on the opposite side from the sidebar. You will be able to move the object vertically within the text page. You also have the option to add a title, introductory text, a border, and a caption for the photo, depending on which design theme you are using; some features may not be available. The "Sidebar" option acts just the same as adding a text box to the sidebar. You may move the object vertically in the sidebar to arrange the page the way you feel is most pleasing.

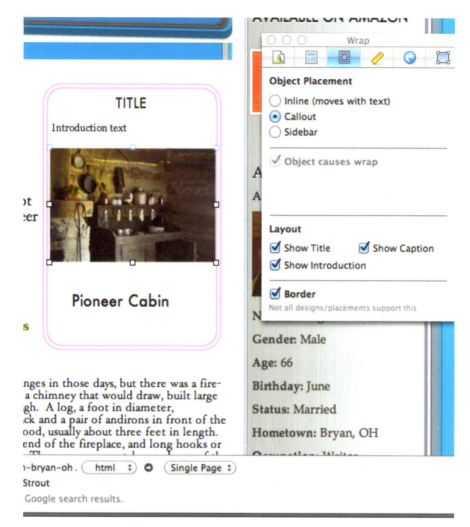

Wrap Inspector with a Sidebar Object

Text inspector appeared in Sandvox® version 2.2 in November, 2011. At this writing, the Text inspector allows you to control and adjust bullet points and numbering of items. Several other text enhancements appear in other areas of Sandvox®, such as the Fonts icon in the menu bar and under Format>Text.

The **Metrics inspector** will show you the size of various objects and pages. Generally, this is a tool for web designers and, if you are a casual user of Sandvox® using pre-designed themes, you may want to leave these settings as they are and explore this feature when you have studied the Designers Guide at Sandvox®'s website.

Link inspector is how you connect your site to other places on the internet as well as linking to email or other pages within your site. The drop down menu is self-explanatory: No link, a link to: another website, a page in your website or to an email address. You can drag and drop, copy and paste a URL into the Link inspector or, if your web browser is on the site you wish to link to, the URL will appear in the box when you choose "External URL" from the link drop down menu. The check box at the bottom of the inspector activates the links in your site so you can test them as you work. They will be active when your site is published.

The **Object inspector** will change depending on the properties of the object you have highlighted. If you are dealing with a Raw HTML object, you will see an "edit HTML" button. This will allow you to make changes to your HTML code such as changing text, font, color or size. Again, practice and experiment before you make any permanent changes.

If the object is a photo, you will see the title, format (jpeg, tiff, etc.) and a space to type in an alternate text for browsers that cannot show the image. The Advanced setting allows you to designate the image as an enclosure for RSS feeds if you are using it in a blog entry that may be going out to subscribers.

5 Exploring Sandvox®: The Top Menu Bar

      The menu bar across the top of the screen looks and functions very much like any other Mac menu bar. There are some Sandvox® specific functions worth noting, however. From left to right, we will review the most important or unique items.

The Sandvox® menu

• About Sandvox® will show you what version you are using.

• Send Feedback will give you a clean email form to pass on your comments to Karelia Software.

• Sandvox® Preferences

    • By loading information from the internet, you will always be working with the current version of your website for editing.

    • Checking the "read URLs" box will make it easier and quicker to create links. When you highlight text, for example, and go to the link inspector tool, choosing link to an external page will automatically insert the page that is currently displayed in the browser.

    • Set the autosave to cycle as often as you want it.

    • Collection URLs: In most cases, the index.html filename is equivalent both ways: http://newname/whatever/ and http://newname/whatever/index.html are the same on most servers.

- Personally, I have the program ask before sending a report to Karelia because some crashes are caused by me and I do not want to send unnecessary reports.
- Unless you are a developer, you would normally want to check for Release versions of software updates.
- The "Show Develop Menu in Menu Bar" option may be interesting to look at but, unless you want to do more advanced web design, it may not be of any use to you. If you check this box a new item appears in the top menu bar which can help with editing HTML.

The next item in the File menu that is unique to Sandvox® is "Choose Comment Provider". You may have already done this under the Page inspector, Appearance tab. Choosing this item will put you in the same place. See Setting up Comments in Chapter 4.

Configure **Google Tools** is also available under the inspector menu and the steps are explained earlier. See the explanation under "The **inspector">document>site.** This is an important aid to generating traffic and tracking how your site is working.

Site Code Injector and **Page Code Injector** under the edit menu, is a powerful and easy tool to modify the site at several different levels. Read the Developer's Guide for more information about this tool. Take the time to learn about HTML and CSS before you make changes to your webpage. Also, validate the code before you publish your page. If you are interested in learning HTML and CSS, there are several online resources.

Visit the following sites for more information:

webmonkey

> http://www.webmonkey.com/2010/02/html_cheatsheet/

HTML code tutor

> http://www.htmlcodetutorial.com/

Insert Menu

The next item across the top bar is the Insert tool. The options here allow you to add a new page at the end of your website. You can drag and move it to a different place in the content outline on the left of your screen.

The **Insert>Text Box** option actually gives you two choices for positioning a text box. If you are working on a page with a sidebar, the new text box will appear at the top of the sidebar column. You can then position it anywhere you want in the sidebar and even deselect it or any other sidebar item using the **Page>Appearance** inspector tool.

If you would like to have a text box that stands alone on the page, you will need to uncheck the Sidebar option in the inspector first. While the sidebar is unchecked in the Appearance inspector tool, adding a text box will cause it to appear on the opposite side of the web page from where the sidebar normally resides in that particular theme. For example, if the sidebar would be on the left, the text box will appear on the right side of the page while the sidebar is unchecked. Having a stand alone text box can be useful to highlight some important information. You can place text, photos, HTML snippets or insert objects such as the IM object. This is a place to exercise your creativity.

If you want both a text box on one side and the sidebar on the other side, select the insert **Text Box** first; then, select the **sidebar** option from the appearance inspector tool. You will now have a three column page, sidebar, body and additional column with text box, also called the "Callout" column.

Insert>Media Placeholder will allow you to easily add music, a photo or videos to your page. You can position it wherever you want by using the wrap inspector tool. If you choose "callout" the placeholder will be on the opposite side from the sidebar. "Inline" will position the placeholder in the body of the page. Of course, choosing "Sidebar" will place the image or other media item at the top of the sidebar. The exact appearance will vary with the theme you are using.

Insert>Indexes gives you several options. The Archive option will generate an index of your blog posts. The photo grid index creates a graphical index of the website. It allows you to create a photo index that can link to your entire site if you wish. Again, the inspector allows you to customize the contents of the photo grid. For each page on your site, you can choose to have it included in the index or not by checking the box next to "indexes" under **inspector>page>include page in**.

RAW HTML allows you to incorporate HTML snippets in your website which gives you tremendous options to expand the appearance and function of your site. You can add maps, scrolling message bars, countdown timers and many other "bells and whistles" to give your site a polished look.

Under **More**, is a list of more items you can use. If you are an instant messenger, you can add a module that will tell people when you are online. You can also add YouTube videos, and Flickr links to your site. Experiment with the ones that fit your needs. Remember, you can always undo what you just did.

The most notable item under **View** is the Web View option that gives you a chance to see the code that drives your web page. You can go from Standard to HTML and examine the code behind the page you have created. The other items in the top menu are clear and easily understood.

Notes

6 Adding Bells and Whistles

Migrating elements of an existing web page

While iWeb® and Sandvox® appear very similar, there are differences in the way they create web pages. iWeb® creates websites one page at a time; that is why you can use a different theme from one page to another in the same website. Sandvox®, on the other hand, applies design elements across all pages on the website so the same banner and design elements appear on all pages.

Some of the terminology may be different but, for our purposes, we will try to stay with Sandvox® terms. The site outline is the hierarchical menu to the left of the main window in the Sandvox® screen. While iWeb® calls this area the sidebar, it functions the same as the Sandvox® site outline. You will become more comfortable with the terms as you build your pages.

While it is not possible to transfer whole websites from iWeb to Sandvox®, one of the easiest tricks in Sandvox® is transferring your existing web page into your new website. These steps work with any website:

- If you were working in iWeb® to build your old site, be sure you have saved your "old" website to a folder on your computer.

- In your finder, open the iWeb® application and look for the page you want to copy.
- Examine the page you want to migrate and decide what element you want to move to Sandvox®, a block of text, a photo or a logo perhaps.

Iweb® page to migrate

- Choose the text or object you want to transfer and copy it. If it was an HTML Snippet in iWeb®, copy the snippet code.
- In Sandvox®, choose the **New** icon from the menu bar at the top of the Sandvox® window and choose the page layout you want.
- Open the page you want to modify on the Sandvox® site and place your cursor where you want the copied item to appear or insert a new text box or RAW HTML object as needed.
- Use the **Edit>Paste and Match Style** command from the top Menu bar. If the style was accidentally transferred and

you do not want it, use **Format>Clear Style** to revert to the design's default style.

- Once the item appears in your Sandvox® website, go to the page inspector and make any modifications you need to blend the old item into the new site.
- You will find that not all items will transfer directly to Sandvox® and you may have to modify your site in small ways to work in Sandvox®.

> **User Tip:** If you choose to move your iWeb site to a new hosting service, remember that whatever your site name is in the publishing setup window of iWeb will become part of the new URL. For example, if you name your site Whatzit, the URL will be something like www.yourdomainname.Whatzit.welcome.html.

Adding New Designs

Even though you have over 60 designs and variations to choose from, there is always room for more options. One source of new designs and design ideas is built into Sandvox®.

- In the top menu bar, select "Sandvox®" and go down to the third item, **Discover Plug-ins**.
- When you choose this option, it will open a new window that lists many of the available add-ons to Sandvox®. Some of these are free and some have a small charge, usually less than $12.95.

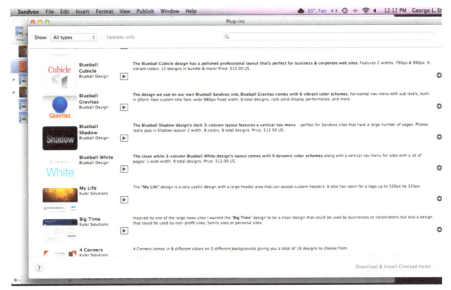

Discover Plug-ins window

• When you find the ones you want, download and install them into the Sandvox application.

Adding Snippets

Snippets are small pieces of HTML code that can add interesting items or functions to your site. Included here is a snippet for a Google search window. You can copy this code into an HTML object on your page. You will discover many different snippets as you explore the web. I have included links to useful websites such as Polldaddy where you can sign up for a free account to create polls on your blog. http:// polldaddy.com/signup-free/

Google search window

This code will add a google search box to your website.

```
<!-- Search Google -->
<center>
<FORM method=GET action="http://www.google.com/search">
<input type=hidden name=ie value=UTF-8>
<input type=hidden name=oe value=UTF-8>
<TABLE bgcolor="#FFFFFF"><tr><td>
<A HREF="http://www.google.com/">
<IMG SRC="http://www.google.com/logos/Logo_40wht.gif"
border="0" ALT="Google" align="absmiddle"></A>
<INPUT TYPE=text name=q size=25 maxlength=255 value="">
<INPUT type=submit name=btnG VALUE="Google Search">
</td></tr></TABLE>
</FORM>
</center>
<!-- Search Google -->
```

Here is another snippet that you can copy from this book or from the website below. This is basic HTML and you can experiment with changing the color or bgcolor values and type in your own message. This is a good code to try for your first HTML snippet to customize your site.

```
<!-- Scrolling sign -->

<div align="center"><FONT
color="0000FF" size="+10"><MARQUEE bgcolor="FFF8DC"
direction="left" loop="true" width=90%"><STRONG>Enter
your text here!</STRONG></MARQUEE></FONT></DIV>

<!-- Scrolling sign-->
```

To get this code on line, go to
http://glstrout.net/sandvox-toys.html

Here is another snippet that embeds a video into your web
page.

```
<object width="640" height="360"><param name="movie"
value="http://www.youtube.com/v/
G9-78a_lnBA&rel=0&hl=en_US&feature=player_embedded&v
ersion=3"></param><param name="allowFullScreen"
value="true"></param><param name="allowScriptAccess"
value="always"></param><embed src="http://
www.youtube.com/v/
G9-78a_lnBA&rel=0&hl=en_US&feature=player_embedded&v
ersion=3" type="application/x-shockwave-flash"
allowfullscreen="true" allowScriptAccess="always"
width="640" height="360"></embed></object>
```

This is a promotional video for a car company that they
are happy to have you share since it spreads the word about
their product.

If you want to learn more about HTML and CSS, go to
http://www.htmlcodetutorial.com/

These are just a few examples of items you can add to
your site. There are many other snippets available on the
web. Experiment and try different ones to spice up your site.
Remember, you can always undo anything you try.

Adding a page using Choose...

This option opens a Finder window to allow you to choose a file to add to your site. One of the extreme uses for this is to migrate content from your old site to your new one. Go to the **New** menu heading and scroll down to **Choose...** This option for adding a new page is very powerful and convenient, especially if you are trying to migrate your old iWeb® to a new Sandvox® site. The following example will demonstrate the power of this feature.

• You will need to edit and correct some items on the page. For example, the menu bar from the old website will still link to the old website and you will need to delete it. The easiest way is to edit the original page and save it to your computer; then follow these steps.

• Under **New**, scroll down to **Choose...** A file browser window will open to show you the files on your computer.

• Find an HTML file in the files containing your old website such as "Links.html".

• Click on the **Insert** button and the entire page will appear in your Site Outline.

• Using the **inspector tool**, you can give the page a name that appears in the menu.

While this can be a quick way to add some content, in most cases, it will give you a more professional site if you create the page entirely in the new theme and copy and paste the individual elements from the old site to the new one.

Notes

7 Editing a published site

After you have published your site, making changes and updating information is easy. You will continue to use the Sandvox® application to keep your visitors interested and up to date through your website. If you have new products to announce or you make regular entries in your blog, you can do this through Sandvox®.

Open your Sandvox® program and choose the icon for your website that you have already published. After it publishes your site, Sandvox® will always ask you if you want to save the changes. By choosing **Save**, you will always have the latest copy of your site on your computer and available to work on in Sandvox®.

As you study your website, you will, no doubt, want to make changes and updates over time. Go back to the Sandvox® app on your computer and revise and edit as you want; then save and publish the changes. Now, when you visit your site live on the Internet, you will see the revised web pages.

Advertising on your website

There are many opportunities for providing support for your website. Even though you will have only minimal costs involved by designing and maintaining your site yourself, you can use advertising to defray the costs. Most places that advertise pay on the basis of "click through" which means you receive a small commission when someone responds to an ad on your site.

Perhaps the most popular advertiser is Amazon.com. By signing up as an Amazon Associate, you can place banners on your site that will give you the opportunity to promote various products sold on Amazon. Go to Amazon.com at https://affiliate-program.amazon.com/ for more information.

Another option to consider is Google AdSense which sets up advertising tied to the content of your web page. You can get more information at https://www.google.com/adsense/support/bin/answer.py?answer=79985&sourceid=aso&medium=link&subid=ww-ww-et-logoutdemo

Both of these sources are quick and easy to set up and maintain.

8 Blogs, Podcasts and Videos

Adding New Blog Entries

As a blogger, you will want to stay current with your blog. Family, friends or business associates and customers will come to rely on your blog for the latest information on your products or activities. Try to establish a regular schedule for updates and new entries so your readers know when to expect news.

On the front page of your new blog, give a summary of the purpose and intent of your blog so that the visitor knows what to expect. In subsequent entries, try to stay close to your stated purpose for the blog. If you are doing a blog that is supposed to be "all about creative writing," try to stay with the topic. If you feel you have something important to say on another subject, begin the entry with a note that this entry will be "off topic." If you find you are writing off topic often, either redefine your purpose or consider starting a separate blog.

Go to the **Page inspector> Collection** to establish your settings for your blog. Choose the setting you like. Experiment until you are satisfied with the appearance of your blog; then save the changes. In most cases, do not change the filename; the default will work fine and avoid errors.

To add an entry to your blog, highlight the main blog page in the Site Outline; then go to **New>Empty/Text** or **Empty/Text-without sidebar**. The new blank page will appear under the main page of your blog and in your main Sandvox® window. You are now ready to type your title and entry. After you finish your entry, go to **Publish** in the Menu and your new blog post will be uploaded to your site. When the process is finished, Sandvox® will ask if you want to save the changes. Choose **Save** and you have finished your latest blog post. If you are not finished with your writing and want to come back and work on it later, go to **Page inspector>Page** and choose the first check box **Draft** and the page will not be published until you are ready and have unchecked the box.

These same options are available for any collections such as photo albums you create but are not yet ready to publish.

Adding Podcasts, Music and Videos

To add a Podcast, song or video, open the Media browser in Sandvox® and choose the podcast, song or video you want to add to your web page. Drag and drop it on the page. Once it appears on the page, click on the image of the object you have added. You can now move it where you want on the page. Open the inspector tool and go to the **Wrap inspector**. From here you can choose placement options: **Inline** (with left, center or right placement), **Callout**, and **Sidebar**. You can try the different placements and decide what looks best for your site.

Now click on the **Media** inspector, the last symbol in the top of the inspector tool bar. Your options will change depending on which media type you are working with at the time. You can choose the settings that you prefer. The one setting you always choose is under Advanced; check the box beside "**Copy file into document**" to make the object operate more consistently.

Copyright

A reminder: you are publishing to the internet when you post your website. Follow the rules for intellectual property and do not post anything that is restricted or plagiarized. Be sure you either have permission, own the original material or the item you post is in the public domain. When in doubt, do not post it.

Notes

9 Setting up a Hosting Service

At the end of Chapter One, we briefly reviewed the process of setting up a hosting service. In most cases, the process is simple and easy to accomplish. Follow the guide provided by the hosting service.

When you first contact the hosting service, have a domain name in mind and verify that it is available. In most cases you can order the domain name directly through the hosting service. Keep the name simple, easy to remember and descriptive.

As of this writing, this is a list of ten hosting services with their links:

- iPower   http://www.ipower.com/ipower/index.bml
- GreenGeeks http://www.greengeeks.com/
- Inmotion http://www.inmotionhosting.com/
- Hub http://www.webhostinghub.com/
- HostPapa http://www.webhostinghub.com/
- Hostmonster http://www.hostmonster.com/
- Bluehost http://www.bluehost.com/
- Justhost http://www.justhost.com/
- Fatcow http://www.fatcow.com/
- Ipage http://www.ipage.com/ipage/index.html

This list is offered as a resource and does not constitute an endorsement of any particular site. Take a little time to explore the hosting service site and get a feel for how helpful and friendly they are. There are certain to be times when you will need their help to fix or understand some element. If you do not feel comfortable contacting them for help, go to another service. Compare pricing and packages; while they may seem very similar on the surface, there can be additional prices for some features on some hosting services. The annual cost can run from a few dollars to a few hundred dollars from service to service. When you have made your choice, register and open your account.

Once you register, go to CPanel, or control panel, and follow the "Getting Started Wizard" or whatever that service calls its startup guide. The guide should lead you through an easy startup process. In the end you will want an FTP or SFTP connection for uploading and updating your site.

FTP Accounts

Sandvox® provides a publishing setup which includes the tools for uploading your website to the internet. Consult with your hosting service to get the protocol you will need to select. The hosting service is your best guide on this. If you need to use FTP to upload files to your site, you will need to create an FTP account. You can do this in the FTP Account area that is on the publish setup page of Sandvox®. The hosting service should be able to help you establish the connection.

Now that you have a working web site, you may want to expand and update it. To keep it current, check with the Karelia Blog for more ideas and suggestions from other users and check my website for new entries.

http://www.karelia.com/news/

http://glstrout.net/using-sandvox.html

Also, you can register your site with Karelia so that others can see your work. This will help drive traffic to your site. As you become more involved in the Sandvox community, you will have many other ideas. Enjoy the fun of creating and expanding your own web site.

Notes

About the author

George L. Strout has worked on personal computers for over twenty-five years. This is his second book in a series of Web Design guides. His purpose is to give non-programmers an easy and inexpensive way to create and maintain their own website. He has also written articles and is currently working on several writing projects including the third book in this series.

You can contact the author at george@glstrout.net or visit his websites, created with Sandvox® at http://glstrout.net/ .

Check for new ideas and code at the *Sandvox Toys!*® website at http://glstrout.net/sandvox-toys.html

A note from the author.

While I am not specifically endorsing any product, this book reflects my personal experience during this project.

When you finish your new site, go to the Sandvox® Registry and submit your site for listing by Sandvox®. http://www.sandvoxsites.com/

www.ingramcontent.com/pod-product-compliance
Lightning Source LLC
Chambersburg PA
CBHW041144050326
40689CB00001B/473